The Kids Book of
ABORIGINAL PEOPLES
in Canada

WRITTEN BY

"lhek'atem" Diane Silvey

ILLUSTRATED BY

John Mantha

KIDS CAN PRESS

To the Elders, who kept the flame of justice burning against all odds. — D.S.

Consultants

The publisher and author wish to express their gratitude and appreciation to the following people for their reviews of the text and/or art. While every effort has been made to ensure accuracy, any errors are the responsibility of the author and publisher.

Northwest Coast: Alan Hoover, retired Curator of Ethnology, Royal British Columbia Museum; Bruce Miller, Department of Anthropology and Sociology, University of British Columbia

Plateau: Alan Hoover, retired Curator of Ethnology, Royal British Columbia Museum; Nicholette Prince, Curator of Plateau Ethnology, Canadian Museum of Civilization

Plains: Arni Brownstone, Assistant Curator, Anthropology Department, Royal Ontario Museum

Arctic: Sue Rowley, Curator, Museum of Anthropology, University of British Columbia

Subarctic: Judy Thompson, Curator of Western Subarctic Ethnology, Canadian Museum of Civilization

Iroquoians of the Eastern Woodlands: Cath Oberholtzer, Anthropology Department, Trent University; Judy Hall, Curator of Eastern Woodlands Ethnology, Canadian Museum of Civilization; David Newhouse, Native Studies Department, Trent University

Algonquians of the Eastern Woodlands: Cath Oberholtzer, Anthropology Department, Trent University

First paperback edition 2012

Kids Can Press acknowledges the financial support of the Government of Ontario, through the Ontario Media Development Corporation's Ontario Book Initiative; the Ontario Arts Council; the Canada Council for the Arts; and the Government of Canada, through the BPIDP, for our publishing activity.

Published in Canada by
Kids Can Press Ltd.
25 Dockside Drive
Toronto, ON M5A 0B5

Published in the U.S. by
Kids Can Press Ltd.
2250 Military Road
Tonawanda, NY 14150

www.kidscanpress.com

Edited by Valerie Wyatt
Designed by Julia Naimska
Drum painting on p.5 by Joe Silvey

The hardcover edition of this book is smyth sewn casebound.
The paperback edition of this book is limp sewn with a drawn-on cover.
Manufactured in Tseung Kwan O, NT Hong Kong, China, in 5/2012 by Paramount Printing Co. Ltd.

CM 05 0 9 8 7 6 5
CM PA 12 0 9 8 7 6 5 4 3 2 1

Library and Archives Canada Cataloguing in Publication

Silvey, Diane
The kids book of Aboriginal peoples in Canada / written by Diane Silvey ; illustrated by John Mantha.

ISBN 978-1-55074-998-4 (bound)   ISBN 978-1-55453-930-7 (pbk.)

1. Native peoples — Canada — History — Juvenile literature.
2. Native peoples — Canada — Social life and customs — Juvenile literature.
I. Mantha, John II. Title.

E78.C2S546 2012   j971.004'97   C2011-908281-0

Kids Can Press is a **corus** Entertainment company

CONTENTS

INTRODUCTION

From time immemorial, Canada has been the home of a varied population of Aboriginal peoples. On the west coast, Aboriginal peoples built massive plank houses, each capable of housing sixty people or more.

On the plains, the peoples hunted buffalo and used the animal for food, shelter, clothing and tools. In the eastern woodlands, six nations joined together to form a powerful confederacy, the earliest government in Canada.

In all, there were seven major groups of Aboriginal peoples.

The seven main cultural groups of Canada's Aboriginal peoples were:

- Northwest Coast
- Plateau
- Plains
- Arctic
- Subarctic
- Woodland Iroquoians
- Woodland Algonquians

Where Did the Aboriginal Peoples Come From?

Some people believe that a land bridge joining North America to Asia emerged when the sea level dropped during an ice age. Asian people may have crossed over this bridge into the Arctic and spread from there throughout all of North America.

However, most Aboriginal peoples believe they originated here in North America. The Seneca story of creation tells how a chief's pregnant wife fell through a hole in the sky to the sea below, landed on a turtle's back (the land) and gave birth to the Seneca people. The Mi'kmaq tell of a creator named Gisoolg, who created the animals, birds and plants

in their land and used a bolt of lightning to shape a human being out of sand. This first person was known as Glooscap. The Haudenosaunee tell of a visiting spirit from Sky World who placed them where they are, gave them their names (Cayuga, Ganiengehaga, Oneida, Onondaga, Seneca) and agricultural gifts, such as beans, squash and corn.

Different Yet the Same

Just as Aboriginal peoples had different stories to explain how they came to be here, they also had unique and distinct cultures (ways of living). *Where* they lived played an important role in *how* they lived.

In the eastern woodlands, where trees were abundant, they built villages of longhouses. On the plains, the people erected tipis made of buffalo hide and poles. These tipis could be taken down and easily transported as they moved. In the Arctic, where building materials are hard to find, the people cleverly used snow blocks to build their winter houses.

Despite their differences, all Aboriginal peoples shared, and continue to share, deep roots in the past and sacred values of respect, balance and harmony. These values are passed on from one generation to the next by the elders. They tell the children stories that provide examples of how one should act toward others, with honour and respect, as well as how to respect the land, plants and animals. Elders are respected in Aboriginal society. They serve as role models for the young by demonstrating harmony, balance and integrity in their daily lives and respect towards all things.

Past and Present

In this book, you will first read about the seven main Aboriginal cultural groups and how they lived around the time the Europeans arrived. Then, starting on page 48, you will see what happened to Aboriginal peoples as they came into contact with European explorers, traders and settlers.

"Contact" brought diseases, an end to traditional practices and Aboriginal languages and the disintegration of family life. Later, discriminatory laws were passed to assimilate the Aboriginal people — to make them blend in with European-Canadians. Many hard years followed as Aboriginal people struggled to maintain and rebuild their identity. The last section of this book looks at those struggles and triumphs.

Even after repeated attempts to make them more like non-Aboriginal Canadians, many Aboriginal people have never given up their traditional values and customs, which are still being practised today.

Names

We have made every attempt to use the correct names of the peoples, rather than names given to them by others. For example, on the northwest coast, the early Europeans called the Nuu-chah-nulth people "Nootka." That name lasted for many years. In this book we use the names the peoples call themselves. At the start of each section we also show the names they were once called by others, like this: Nuu-chah-nulth (Nootka).

Places

The maps in this book show the territories of Aboriginal peoples in Canada. But there were no firm boundaries, and groups moved over time and their locations often shifted.

Time

This book shows life around the time of contact with people coming from Europe. The information and pictures are based on artifacts that have survived (such as tools and clothing), on some of the early paintings and descriptions of the Europeans and on other research.

Respect

Generosity

Honour

Spirituality

Integrity

Sharing

Wisdom

Balance

PEOPLES OF THE NORTHWEST COAST

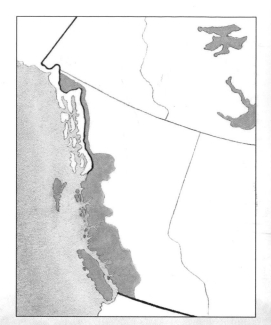

A narrow strip of land between British Columbia's Coast Mountains and the Pacific Ocean was, and still is, home to the peoples of the Northwest Coast, a rich and varied group of cultures and languages.

The terrain is rugged, with thick undergrowth on the forest floor. The coastline is broken up by bays, inlets, deep channels and islands. Dense stands of Douglas fir, Sitka spruce, western hemlock and western red cedar trees thrive in the wet climate. Food, building materials and other natural resources were abundant in many parts of the Northwest Coast. The Fraser River was especially rich in fish. The peoples of the Northwest Coast built elaborate permanent villages and carved massive totem poles, sea-going canoes and ceremonial masks. They held potlatches and other ceremonies in which dances and singing played a specific role. The peoples who lived here were rich, materially and spiritually.

Villages ranged in size from seven to thirty houses, with two hundred to a thousand people in all. The village was built along a shore or river. When selecting a site, the chief considered its position in case of attack and made sure it was close to fresh drinking water. The pictures you see here show a northern style of houses and canoes on page 6 and a southern style on page 7.

Totem poles were carved to serve different purposes. There were several kinds. Clan or family poles had figures or animals, such as Bear, Wolf, Owl, Killer Whale, Eagle and Thunderbird. Mortuary poles often had a grave box at the top. The box held an important person's remains. Memorial poles were raised in memory of a dead chief. There were also shaming and welcoming poles.

Peoples of the Northwest Coast

Coast Salish	Nuxalk (Bella Coola)
Nuu-chah-nulth (Nootka)	Tsimshian
Kwakwaka'wakw (Kwakiutl)	Nisga'a
Haisla	Gitxsan
Heiltsuk (Bella Bella)	Haida
Owekeeno	Tlingit

Fish was the main food, but other animals were hunted, too. Goats, mountain goats, bears, deer, beavers, raccoons and waterfowl were plentiful, as were sea mammals, including whales, seals, sea lions and sea otters.

Some houses were massive — 160 m x 20 m (525 ft. x 65 ft.). A house was occupied by an extended family of thirty to sixty people.

Canoes plied a never-ending water highway. The largest ones could hold forty to fifty men and travel 1500 km (930 mi.). It took a skilled craftsman to build a large, seaworthy freight or war canoe without the aid of blueprints. After the canoe was completed, a ceremony was sometimes held and a name bestowed on the canoe.

The work was divided between the men and women. The men hunted, fished, traded, logged trees, built houses and canoes, and made fishing implements, tools and a variety of carved items. The women gathered plants, shellfish and berries. They wove blankets, mats, capes, hats and skirts, cooked and preserved food and looked after the children.

Cedar — The Tree of Life

The cedar was truly a tree of life to the peoples of the Northwest Coast. It provided them with houses, canoes, totem poles, clothing and the other items you see here.

The people showed profound respect for the cedar tree. Before taking any part of a tree, a person placed both hands on the trunk and said a prayer of thanks to the tree for giving freely of itself. The goal was to use only what was needed and preserve the tree. So, when women stripped bark, they left the tree itself otherwise unharmed. Similarly, the men cut large house planks out of a standing tree while taking care not to kill the tree. The cedar tree held both cleansing and spiritual properties. The branches, for example, were used for "brushing off" — both cleansing and taking away the bad spirits.

The women gathered cedar bark. After a prayer, a slit was made near the bottom of the tree. Then a woman grasped the bark firmly with both hands and started walking backwards. As she did so, a strip of bark tore evenly up the length of the tree.

The cedar bark was collected, folded into bundles and transported home. There, the bark was soaked and then beaten to make it soft and pliable for weaving. Woven cedar clothing felt much like soft sheep's wool, but it was water repellent.

Weaving

Many groups were superb weavers. This Chief Maquinna hat, named after a Nuu-chah-nulth chief, was crafted out of cedar bark, spruce root and surf grass. It has a very distinctive conical shape that narrows at the top then flares out into an onion-shaped bulb. Whale designs were often woven into the work.

Bentwood Boxes

Ingenious woodworking techniques were needed to make a bentwood box. Three planks of cedar were used — two for the top and bottom and the other for the sides. The side plank was scored and steamed so that it could be bent into a box shape, which was held secure by rope until the wood dried. The finished box was pegged or sewn together. Bentwood boxes were used to cook in, to store special items or as burial boxes.

Carved Items

Bowls, paddles, cradles, burial boxes and headpieces were carved out of cedar and other woods. The carver decorated these objects with animal or human figures.

Bark Rope and Twine

Cedar withes (the flexible young branches of cedar trees) were prepared, twisted into a thickness of two or three plies and then braided. Braided cedar was made into many things from rope and fishing line to nets.

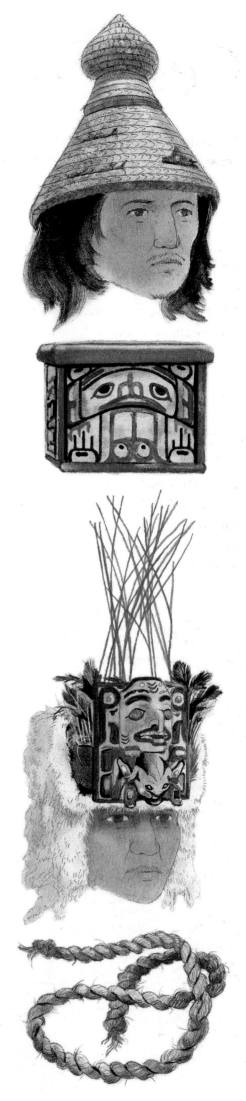

Ceremonies

On the Northwest Coast, the potlatch was, and still is, an important ceremony for a number of peoples. It was an event where spiritual and political events were witnessed. It was also a place and time to commemorate births, deaths, marriages, puberty and the receiving of a title or name.

Several hundred people gathered for a potlatch that could last several days. There would be dancing, singing, feasting and the distribution of gifts, such as blankets and bentwood boxes. The House Speaker was an important person at the potlatch. It was his duty to memorize the names, dances, history and traditions of the people. This knowledge he passed down orally to younger generations.

The Shaman

A shaman had supernatural powers to heal the sick, predict future events and assist the warriors when they went on raids. The shaman performed healing ceremonies publicly, accompanied by singing and drumming.

Men or women could become shamans. To do so, they had to undergo a gruelling regime of fasting, bathing and beating their bodies to become ritually clean and so gain the aid of a supernatural helper.

Masks

During the winter, supernatural beings or spirits were known to visit villages, and it was a time for feasting, dancing and singing. For some groups it was also a time for initiation into secret societies.

A variety of masks were worn to represent the supernatural beings or animals who had arrived from dwelling places in caves, forests, under water or in the sky. Most dramatic was the transformation mask. An outer casing of a bird might conceal a human-like mask underneath. By pulling a set of strings, the dancer opened the outer bird mask to reveal another spirit beneath.

Musical instruments

During ceremonies, rattles served as a link to the world of the supernatural and were used to signal the presence of spirits. Rattles were carved out of wood or made from shells or deer hoofs. Planks or hollow objects, such as cedar boxes, were used as drums.

A bird rattle

A cedar box drum

A fishing weir

Food

The peoples of the Northwest Coast were skilled fishermen. They had sophisticated traps, nets and weirs (fence-like devices set across a river to trap fish). Fishing was a family affair. The father caught the fish, the mother prepared the catch and the children learned adult skills as they helped. Enough fish had to be smoked or dried to last the entire village through the winter. In some areas, salmon was the staple; in others, halibut.

A number of secondary fish were also caught, such as herring, smelt, ling cod, sturgeon and eulachon. Eulachon were boiled down into a valuable oil. The oil was a delicacy — food was dipped into it to add flavour. Eulachon oil was in high demand and was traded with the peoples living inland. The trails used by the traders have been dubbed "grease trails" because of the oil. It has been said that the eulachon were so full of oil that if a wick was placed inside one and lit, the fish would burn like a candle. For this reason, eulachon are sometimes called candle fish.

Eulachon

Sea and land mammals were hunted, including mountain goats, bears, beaver and deer, as well as seals, sea lions, whales and sea otters. Waterfowl were also caught.

Food-gathering areas were owned by certain families. During the summer, camas bulbs, ferns and seaweed were gathered. Berries were made into berry cakes and then sun-dried. Young girls accompanied the women, learning what to harvest and where. For example, there are two kinds of camas bulbs — one is edible, the other poisonous. The girls had to learn the difference.

One treat was soopalie. Soap berries, water and some sweet-tasting berries were mixed together, then beaten into a light foam that resembled ice cream.

Clams were also gathered, as were oysters, mussels, abalone, crabs, limpets, periwinkles and sea urchins.

PEOPLES OF THE PLATEAU

Between the Coast Mountains and the Rocky Mountains, in what is now British Columbia, lived the peoples of the Plateau. The land ranged from semi-desert to forests, with mountains and rivers. It was rich in salmon-bearing streams and had subalpine meadows full of plants and animals. Large game, such as deer, moose, elk and mountain goats, were plentiful. People travelled to hunt and to gather plants during the spring, summer and fall and returned to their villages in winter.

The homes of the Plateau peoples depended on the location and time of year. They might be lean-tos, lodges, tents, tipis and semi-underground pit houses like the one you see here. This house would have been used in winter.

Pit houses had a unique dome shape. Only the roof or top part of the house was visible — the bottom part was dug into the earth. A village could have as many as a hundred houses. If you were to come upon an old abandoned village site today, you would find the earth pock-marked by the remains of pit houses.

The roof was a framework of poles covered with boughs and earth. The men and older women entered the house through a hole in the roof and then down a notched log ladder. The roof hole also served as a chimney. The younger women probably entered through a side door.

Clothing

Men and women wore clothing made of tanned hides of deer, caribou and moose. Some Plateau groups made clothing out of woven grasses or the pounded bark of certain types of bushes. Moccasins were made of tanned deer hide or sometimes salmon skins.

During the winter, the people added mittens, hats and robes made from fur or goat wool. Mountain goat robes were sought after because their double coat of dense fur and long guard hairs provided extra insulation from the cold.

Clothing was often decorated with paint, shells, fur and feathers. Garments made for rites-of-passage ceremonies, for shamans or for high-ranking chiefs, warriors or hunters were elaborately decorated.

Several families lived in a house and shared a central cooking fire. Each family's sleeping area was separated from the others by mats woven from rushes.

Food was stored outside in bark-lined pits or on raised storage platforms to keep it away from predators such as bears and wolverines.

Fishing for Salmon

Long ago, the salmon runs drew thousands of people to the rivers of the British Columbia interior. The peoples of the Plateau were skilled and inventive fishermen and used a variety of fishing techniques for different fishing spots and seasonal conditions, such as high or low water. Special fishing rocks or spots were sometimes owned and inherited by families or village groups.

In some areas, fishermen built fishing platforms that jutted out over the rocks along the river's edge. The fisherman would stand on the platform and scoop great amounts of salmon out of the river with long-handled dip nets. Fishermen also used weirs, traps, spears, harpoons and leisters (spears) to catch the salmon.

A fisherman thrusts a harpoon into a salmon. Cords attached to the harpoon heads let the fisherman retrieve the fish.

Preserving the salmon

The village needed to preserve salmon to survive the long months of winter. To prepare the fish, the women cleaned and removed the

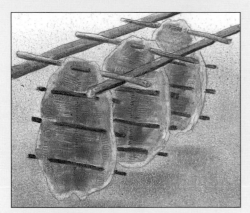

fins, backbone and head. This left a large flank of salmon. Spreaders were used to hold the flank flat, and at the tail a sturdy stick was inserted from which to hang the

fish. The salmon was often dried on a hill where there was plenty of wind, or it might be smoke-cured in a smokehouse.

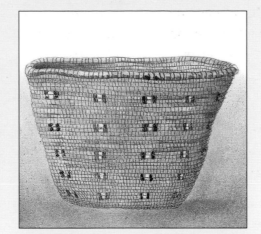

When it was needed, the dried salmon was cooked in watertight baskets. Water was poured into a basket, then hot rocks were taken

out of the fire with tongs and placed in the water. Once the water started to boil, the pieces of salmon were added.

To extract the fishes' oil, the salmon were boiled in pits until the oil rose to the surface of the water and could be skimmed off. The oil was stored for the winter and used as a condiment to dip food into. The salmon could also be dried, roasted and pounded into a coarse powder. The powder was then mixed with salmon oil and Saskatoon berries to make pemmican, a nutritious food that could be transported for eating on the trail. Salmon eggs (roe) were eaten fresh or dried.

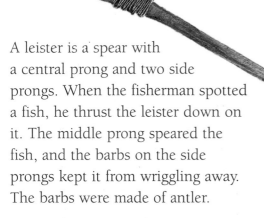

A leister is a spear with a central prong and two side prongs. When the fisherman spotted a fish, he thrust the leister down on it. The middle prong speared the fish, and the barbs on the side prongs kept it from wriggling away. The barbs were made of antler.

Indian hemp plants were gathered, split, dried, beaten, spun and twisted into twine by the women. The men wove the twine into fishing nets and built the frames for dip nets out of young fir trees.

This fish trap was made by the Ktunaxa people. It was used in shallow streams or in connection with a weir (fence-like trap). The fish swam in the open end of the basket and were trapped.

Trade

The Plateau peoples lived in the middle of a trade network that extended from the Northwest Coast peoples to the Plains peoples, southward to The Dalles in what is now Oregon and northwards into today's Alaska.

Groups traded items they had in excess, such as dried salmon, for things they needed. People traded dried berries, skins and mountain goat wool to the people of the Northwest Coast. In return, they got dentalium shells (seashells) and other ocean products.

A sturgeon-nosed canoe

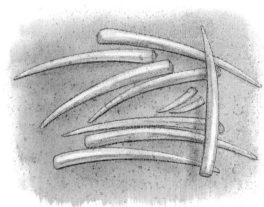

Dentalium shells

Dentalium shells were used for decorations and as a unit of exchange (money). The shells were gathered by the Nuu-chah-nulth people on the west coast of Vancouver Island. They were graded into lengths, with the longer, unbroken ones being most valuable. Through trade, the dentalium shells made their way across a large part of western North America.

Games

A game of balance and concentration was an enjoyable way to pass the time. Two teams of five players faced each other. The players would squat on their heels and sing, clap and hop on the spot. The winning team was the one that had the last upright player.

Transportation

Fast-flowing rivers and rapids meant most travel was done on foot, along well-worn trade routes and trails. Heavy loads were carried on the traveller's back, with the aid of a tumpline (a harness fitted over the forehead). In winter, some groups used snowshoes and toboggans to help them get around.

When water travel was possible, the people used dugout canoes made out of cottonwood, as well as rafts and bull boats. A bull boat looked like a large round bowl made of hide stretched over a wooden frame. The Ktunaxa people built sturgeon-nosed canoes, so-called because of their elongated bow and stern. Traditionally, the canoe was made from six different types of trees — birch, bitter cherry, cedar, Douglas fir, maple and white pine.

Hunting and Gathering

Mule deer, elk, black bears, mountain goats, caribou and bighorn sheep were hunted with bows and arrows, spears and various traps. Deer fences were often used. A rough fence was built to stop the deer from crossing except at certain places, where a trap was hidden. As the deer stepped onto a concealed snare, a rope closed around the animal's feet, trapping it.

Wild plants, including berries, roots, bark, lichen, cactus and nuts, were gathered and preserved for the winter. Women gathered the berries with wooden berry pickers. This flared tool, which resembled an outstretched hand, let them gather the maximum amount of berries in a minimum amount of time. The berries were mashed and dried and turned into fruit leather or cakes. For a sweet treat, the cambium (inner bark) of the jack pine was scraped off, eaten and enjoyed. Wild plants were an important part of the peoples' diet. Medicinal plants were also gathered.

A war club

Warfare

From time to time disputes would break out between groups. Then, a war chief was chosen for both his courage and fighting skills. He would lead a group of warriors in a raid. The warriors wore armour made of wood and elk hide and carried shields for protection. Their weapons included clubs, daggers, spears and bows and arrows.

Art

The Stl'atl'imx and the Nlaka'pamux people were, and still are, well known for their superbly crafted cedar baskets. Made from cedar roots woven tightly and uniformly, the baskets became waterproof once they were soaked in water and the joints swelled. They were used for carrying things and as cooking pots. They were decorated with intricate geometric patterns in black and red.

Seated human figure bowls were sculpted out of soapstone or sandstone. It is thought the bowls may have been used by shamans during puberty rites that marked a young girl's passage into womanhood.

PEOPLES OF THE PLAINS

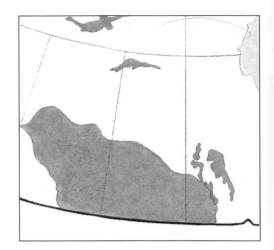

Stretching across Alberta, Saskatchewan and southwestern Manitoba is a windswept prairie. The land is flat and treeless, with a few rolling hills and steep cliffs. Tall prairie grass or short grass once covered most of the land. Three major rivers flow through — the Bow, Assiniboine and the South Saskatchewan. This land was, and still is, the Canadian territory of the peoples of the Plains.

During the winter, small bands of people lived in protected valleys away from the strong north winds. Soon after the arrival of spring, the peoples became nomadic in their quest for food. They roamed the prairies, searching for the great herds of migrating buffalo.

The peoples travelled in small groups except when they came together for communal hunts or ceremonies. Tipis were the ideal homes — they were easy to transport and set up as the groups moved from place to place.

Tipis were made, owned and set up by the women. A conical framework of pine poles was erected and tied at the top. Then a buffalo hide covering was draped around the frame and tied to the top. The ends of the cover came together above the doorway, where they were secured together with wooden pins.

The tipi was anchored to the ground with sturdy wooden pegs and rocks to keep it from blowing over in high winds.

To transport their goods, including tipis, from place to place, the people piled them on a travois. This V-shaped frame was made by lashing together two pine poles. The travois was harnessed to a dog or, later, a horse.

Women and children gathered wild food plants such as berries, bitterroot, camas and wild turnips. These were eaten fresh or preserved for the winter.

The men hunted with spears, snares and bows and arrows. They looked for pronghorn antelope, mule deer, elk and prairie chickens to add to their food supplies. But their staple was buffalo meat.

Clothing

Clothing was made from buffalo, deer, elk or antelope hide. The women first scraped and tanned the hide, then sewed the pieces together with buffalo sinew. Clothes were decorated with dyed porcupine quills and were often fringed. A robe of warm buffalo hide helped in the bitter cold. Below are pictures of Siksika clothing.

The Buffalo Hunters

The Plains peoples depended on the buffalo, or "bison," to provide them with food, clothing, housing, weapons, fuel, transportation, containers and tools.

At one time, more than fifty million buffalo roamed the plains of North America. Each year a communal hunt was planned. The rules of the hunt were strictly enforced — if an over-eager hunter spooked the herd before the given signal, the hunt could fail and the whole camp would face starvation. The buffalo hunt was crucial to the survival of the group.

One method of hunting was to herd the buffalo into a pound, which is an enclosed area much like a corral. There, the hunters would dispatch the animals with spears.

Another method involved the use of buffalo jumps, such as the one at Head-Smashed-In Buffalo Jump in Alberta. The hunters would chase a herd towards a cliff, causing them to panic, stampede over the edge and fall to their death.

The introduction of the horse in the 1700s gave the hunters a huge advantage. They could now ride after a buffalo and bring it down with a well-aimed arrow.

The buffalo

A full-grown bull (male) buffalo stands up to 2 m (6 1/2 ft.) tall and weighs up to 700 kg (1540 lb.). It was the women's job to turn the bison into food and other essentials of life. The meat was dried slowly and made into pemmican — enough to last the village through the winter. Here are some of the other ways the Plains peoples used the buffalo.

Hide: clothing, bags, tipi covers, drums, bull boat covers, shields, blankets, robes

Bones: war clubs, tools, knives, awls, scrapers, arrowheads, sleds

Sinew: thread

Horns: drinking cups, spoons, headdresses

Tail: whisks

Bladder: water containers

Dung: fuel

Hair: rope

Tongue: food

Hooves: rattles, glue

Stomach sack: cooking pots (Hot stones were dropped into the sack, causing the water inside to boil and cook the food.)

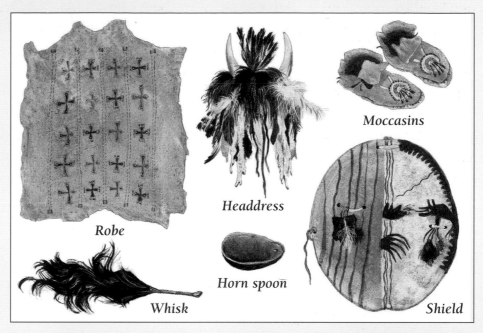

Robe

Headdress

Moccasins

Whisk

Horn spoon

Shield

Trade

Catlinite (a red clay) was a highly prized trade item used to make tobacco pipes. The clay came from a quarry in Minnesota. The quarry was a sacred place, and all people entering or leaving the site had to do so in peace. The Plains peoples in Canada traded their excess buffalo meat or other buffalo products for catlinite. At times, they made the journey to Minnesota to obtain the clay for themselves. The people carried their pipes and tobacco in embroidered leather bags.

Tobacco pipe

Warfare

The Blackfoot Confederacy consisted of a number of nations — the Siksika, Kainai, Pikuni and, for a time, the Tsuu T'ina and A'aninin. Although

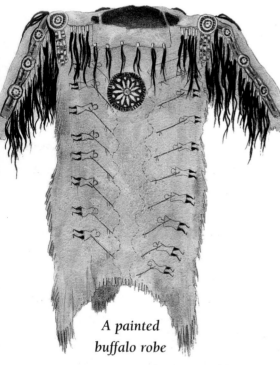

A painted buffalo robe

each group was independent of the others, collectively they made a powerful alliance that wielded control over a large portion of the plains. They launched war parties against their enemies.

A war chief was chosen for his bravery and skill. He led his warriors in surprise raids against enemy camps. The warriors wielded spears, knives, clubs and bows and arrows, and carried shields made of buffalo hide to protect themselves.

War was a way for men to gain prestige and honour, especially by daring feats, such as snatching an enemy's weapon during battle. These war deeds would be told and retold for years, adding to the warrior's reputation. A distinguished warrior had his war exploits painted onto a buffalo robe, which he would display for all to witness.

Games

Plains children learned about the life they would lead as grown-ups through play.

Very young girls had birch dolls made for them by the adults. These dolls might be as simple as a birch stick with a whittled head and shoulders. The girl would wrap the doll with buckskin to clothe it.

Older girls had more elaborate toys. Small versions of a travois let girls practise how to move camp. The travois would be loaded with miniature household materials. Making tiny tipis taught girls skills they would later use to erect full-sized ones.

Gathering for the Sun Dance

Ceremonies

During the summer, groups of Plains people gathered to participate in the Sun Dance, a ceremony that was at the heart of their culture. First, a central pole was erected, then a circular Sun Dance Lodge was constructed around the pole. Sacred offerings, such as tobacco, were placed on the pole. Within the sacred circle, a painted buffalo skull was laid in a place of honour. The sacred Sun Lodge was surrounded by tipis. The painted tipis in the inner circle belonged to the leaders.

The Sun Dance went on for several days. It was a time for individuals to commune with the spirits. The Dance strengthened their beliefs and gave these nomadic people an opportunity to come together and reforge family ties and friendships.

The dancers made themselves ritually clean by fasting, dancing and praying to the Great Spirit. Some of the dancers endured pain as part of the Sun Dance, not as a sign of bravery but as a sacrifice to the Creator.

During the Sun Dance, sacred bundles or medicine bundles were opened. The objects inside were special and sacred to the individual.

Dance belt

Tobacco

The Siksika cultivated tobacco and smoked it for pleasure and to mark important events, treaties and agreements. The tobacco was also used for special ceremonies. The smoke acted as a path through which a person's prayers ascended from the physical world to the spirit world.

Eagle Feathers

Eagles were and are highly respected in many Aboriginal cultures. The Plains peoples used eagle feathers in their ceremonies and dances.

To capture an eagle, a pit was dug, baited with food and then camouflaged with leaves and sticks. The hunter waited patiently for an eagle to land and be trapped. Because eagles were sacred, the hunter would perform a ritual and pray for the dead eagle.

The eagle feathers were made into a number of items, including headdresses, fans and belts and bustles worn by dancers at ceremonial events.

PEOPLES OF THE ARCTIC

The Arctic is mostly tundra — treeless land where only the topmost layer of soil thaws enough for shrubs, lichen and plants to grow in summer. Under this layer is permafrost — a mixture of soil, silt and gravel that is permanently frozen.

In summer the days are long, with almost twenty-four hours of daylight. In the middle of winter, the sun doesn't rise above the horizon, and the days are very short. Cold, ice and snow are the rule for over half the year.

The peoples who lived here, and still do, are the Inuit and the Inuvialuit. They were skilled and inventive hunters and gatherers who lived in family groups that valued co-operation and sharing.

The igloo was used through most of the Canadian Arctic in winter — snow was the most readily available building material. It was best to use snow that had fallen all at one time, rather than snow from different storms. (Different snowfalls form layers that make the blocks likely to crumble.)

The snow had to be soft enough to cut into blocks yet compact enough to be moved. Snow blocks were cut with a special snow knife. Each block was carefully cut to fit perfectly to make the dome shape of the house. This skill was passed along from father to son and was learned through watching and practising.

A small igloo that would last for a couple of nights during a hunt or journey could be built in less than an hour. Larger igloos, such as the ones you see here, would house a family or two for up to six weeks. Some families lined the inside of their igloos with skin to make them last even longer.

To keep out the wind, soft snow was packed into the cracks between the blocks.

A slab of freshwater ice or translucent seal gut was made into a windowpane.

In some areas, a large snowhouse might be occupied by two families.

A vent hole called a "qihaq" let heat and smoke escape.

Other homes

As the weather warmed, the igloos began to melt and collapse. During the late spring and summer, the Inuit lived in skin tents. In the fall, they lived in houses built of stone, turf or animal bones covered with skins. They would return to these houses year after year.

Food was cooked in a pot hung over a soapstone lamp (usually containing seal oil). Above the pot was a rack for drying clothes.

Once the key block of snow was inserted in the roof, the igloo was solid — so solid that four men could stand on the roof without it collapsing.

Several igloos built close together formed a snow village. The people in the village were usually an extended family of aunts, uncles, cousins and grandparents. The families might share a communal living area that was used for ceremonies, as well as for socializing, singing, drumming, dancing, games and storytelling. Sometimes the igloos were linked by short passageways.

A sleeping platform was cut from the interior snow blocks or built of raised blocks. Stones, paddles or other materials were laid on the platform. These were covered with a mat made of twigs or whale baleen. Finally, layers of skins were placed on top to create a warm mattress. At bedtime the family would sleep in caribou-skin sleeping bags.

A low tunnel served as the entranceway. Inside the dome, air warmed by body heat and the oil lamp would rise. The low tunnel kept this warm air from escaping.

The lamp melted the inner layer of the snow blocks, forming a layer of ice that helped windproof the house.

Hunters of Sea Mammals

Most Inuit groups spent part of the year hunting sea mammals. Seals, walrus and even whales provided the people with oil, thread, skin clothing, boots, storage containers, tools and coverings for boats and tents. All parts of the animals were used — nothing went to waste.

In summer, seals were hunted in the water from kayaks. The hunter would throw a harpoon attached to a float (a seal-skin balloon full of air). Dragging the float would tire the seal so that it could be speared.

On the ice in winter, a hunter would search for a seal's breathing hole. He would place a feather above the hole or put a thin bone stick into the hole and wait patiently beside it. When a seal came to the hole the feather or the stick would move and the hunter would quickly thrust the harpoon into the hole.

In spring, seals bask in the sun on the ice. The hunter would crawl forward, pretending to be a seal.

Walrus were important to the Inuit. The tough hides of the walrus made strong ropes, and their ivory tusks were carved into tools and hunting equipment. Hunting a walrus was dangerous. Hunters in kayaks or umiaks (large, flat-bottomed boats covered in skins, which held up to eight men) risked being attacked and even overturned by an irritated walrus.

Catching a large whale, such as a bowhead, meant the entire community had sufficient food for months.

Instead of teeth, some whales have baleen, a plastic-like material that filters their food. From baleen, people made buckets, mattresses, ties for lashing loads and fishing lines.

Toggle Head Harpoons

The toggle head harpoon was a technological masterpiece. It was designed so that once the head entered the seal, tension on the harpoon line made the head swivel sideways, keeping it firmly embedded in the seal.

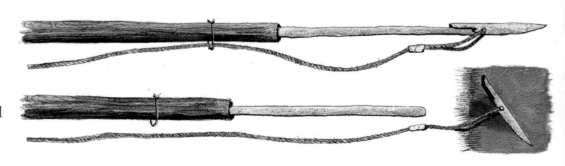

Hunters of the Land

Land animals were important to Inuit groups. They hunted caribou and musk oxen and smaller animals such as hares and ground squirrels.

Many caribou migrate north in summer in large herds. The Inuit waited patiently for the caribou to return along the paths they had followed for years.

Sometimes the Inuit would ambush the caribou as the herd crossed a river. Or they would set up inukshuks (cairns or rock piles) in a V leading to a shallow crossing place or a natural corral. Women and children would stand between the inukshuks and frighten the animals towards the narrow end of the V. As the caribou crossed the river, men in kayaks attacked with spears. Caribou were also stalked and killed with bows and arrows.

Men hunted migrating ducks, geese and guillemots during the summer months. Ptarmigan were hunted all year round. Bird hunters used many methods, including darts mounted on throwing boards, bolas, snares, long-handled nets and bows and arrows. Young boys used slingshots to practise their hunting skills.

The men and older boys fished for Arctic char, whitefish, trout, grayling, turbot and pike. Arctic char and whitefish migrate in great numbers up river in the fall. People built stone weirs (fish traps) and speared great numbers of fish. The women and young girls spent hours preparing the fish for drying and caching (see page 29).

Bolas

One way to hunt birds was with a bola — a bunch of cords tied together, with weights on one end. The hunter would swing the bola over his head like a lasso, then release it into a flock of flying birds.

A bird that was entangled in the bola would fall to the ground.

Young boys practised using a bola to "lasso" a stationary object. Through play, they began to learn hunting skills.

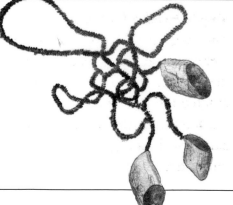

Clothing

Men and women wore a shirt with a hood, pants and boots. In winter a parka was added.

For summer clothing, sealskin was preferred. The skin is full of oil, which makes it water repellent. Sealskin was ideal for kayakers, who wanted to stay dry.

To prepare the skins, the women removed the blubber using an ulu (a semi-circular knife).

Then the skins were stretched, dried, scraped and softened and sewn into clothes. Young girls were taught to sew by their mothers. As they sewed, the mother would pass on not only her knowledge of sewing but also traditional stories.

Survival in the winter depended on staying warm. The caribou skins used for winter clothing (shown above) have two layers of hair that provided wonderful insulation.

Transportation

The peoples of the Arctic moved in search of food in a cycle throughout the year. They might go from the edges of the sea ice, where they hunted in winter, to a river mouth to fish in the spring or hunt caribou in the fall. They took their belongings with them or left them behind in caches. With boats, sleds and on foot, they might travel hundreds of kilometres (miles) a year.

Umiak

This large, flat-bottomed boat with an open top, a sail and paddles were made of wood or bone covered with skin. Umiaks were used by women to transport the family and all their belongings and by men to hunt whales.

Umiak

Kayak

The Inuit developed a highly maneuverable watercraft — the kayak. It was made by stretching and sewing a covering of skin over a framework of light wood, bone or antler.

Kayak

Dog Sledges

Goods were carried on sledges, or sleds. The heavy runners were carved out of wood or whale bone, and their surfaces were covered in a layer of ice and rubbed smooth to glide more easily. Sometimes frozen fish wrapped in skin were used as runners. A team of three to eight dogs pulled the sledge. To protect the dogs' paws from ice crystals during spring melt, the women fitted the dogs with sealskin boots.

Food Caches

Putting food in caches (hiding places) was a way to protect it from predators. Caches were also used to age meat, an Inuit delicacy, and prepare other specialty foods.

There were many styles of caches. Some were pits lined with gravel or stone slabs. They were carefully prepared and often marked with an inukshuk (stone marker). In other places, piles of rock were used. Kayaks and sleds were sometimes cached too.

Inukshuk

An inukshuk is an arrangement of rocks that served as a landmark, a memorial or as an aid in hunting caribou. Today an inukshuk often resembles a human figure, but long ago they were more likely to be just two or three rocks piled one on top of another.

This girl is learning the dog and sled string figure.

Games

For the Inuit, stories served as a means to pass important information from one generation to the next. The children were taught values and traditions as well as useful hunting skills through storytelling. Stories were also entertainment on a long winter's evening.

Many different games, some between two people and some team games, were played. One of these, making string figures, was an enjoyable pastime. A loop of caribou sinew was placed around a person's hands. Using the fingers of both hands, the person wove intricate patterns or figures. There were hundreds of string figures, many with stories or songs.

Spiritual Beliefs

The Inuit believed that everything has a soul, even inanimate objects such as rock outcroppings. Honouring animal spirits was especially important. When an animal was killed, it had to be treated with respect so that it might once again offer itself to the hunter.

Names were sacred. When a person died, their name was given to a newborn baby in the belief that the name-soul of this much-loved person would live again in the child.

The Inuit believed in spirits that controlled aspects of the environment. Most groups believed that the Spirit of the Air controlled the wind and weather, the Spirit of the Sea controlled the sea mammals, and the Spirit of the Moon influenced the movement of land animals.

Shamans

Shamans were people with special powers. They helped cure the sick, interacted with the spirits and predicted the weather, as well as the movements of animals. Shamans could be men or women.

PEOPLES OF THE SUBARCTIC

The Canadian Subarctic stretches across the country from the Labrador coast westward and into northern Canada. This vast area was, and still is, the home of the Subarctic peoples.

Their territory has areas of forest, muskeg, mountains, lakes, rivers and great stretches where no trees grow, called the barren lands. In the summer, black flies and mosquitoes make life difficult for people and animals alike. The winters are harsh — long, dark and extremely cold — and food was often scarce.

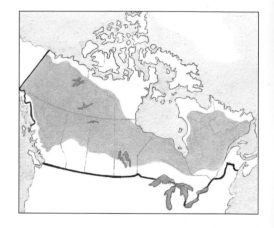

The Subarctic peoples lived in small groups of related families and travelled extensively and in all seasons in search of food and other resources.

Homes varied in style, but all had to be easily transported and assembled. In winter, some groups erected conical tents, while others constructed domed tents like the ones you see

here. Whenever possible, the homes were built in the forest, which provided shelter from the wind, building materials and wood for campfires.

A Gwich'in winter camp

Peoples of the Subarctic

Western Subarctic, speaking
Athapaskan languages:

Tsay Keh Dene (Sekani)
Mountain
Kaska Dena (Kaska)
Tutchone
Tr'ondek Hwech'in (Han)
Gwich'in (Kutchin)
Hare
Dogrib
Yellowknife

Acha-otinne (Slavey)
Dunne-za (Beaver)
Tahltan
Dakelh-ne (Carrier)
Natot'en (Western Carrier)
Wetsuwet'en
Tagish
Chipewyan
Ts'ilh'aot'in (Chilcotin)
Inland Tlingit

Eastern Subarctic, speaking
Algonquian languages:

Subarctic Cree
Attikamek
Innu
Montagnais
Naskapi

Although food was preserved in the summer and fall for the cold months, the men still had to hunt and fish in winter. It was an ongoing struggle to find enough food to survive.

The women cooked meat and fish in water, in containers made of birchbark or caribou skin. Rocks were heated in a fire, then added to the water until it boiled. Meat was then put into the hot water. When meat or fish were in short supply, the people, resourceful as ever, made a thick, nutritious soup out of lichen.

Summer and autumn

Summer was a time for small family groups to converge at good fishing sites. As many as one hundred people might live in a single camp.

They constructed shelters covered with caribou hides or spruce boughs along riverbanks or lakes to take full advantage of any breezes that might help chase away the hordes of mosquitoes and blackflies.

The men built large fish weirs and used nets to trap fish. The women dried and smoked the fish to preserve them for eating later in the year. The women also gathered berries and preserved them by drying them for winter use. The people enjoyed the chance to visit with one another once again and to trade extra goods they had for things they needed.

In the fall the large group broke into smaller family groups and headed to their hunting territories to spend the winter. The men hunted big game animals such as caribou, moose and mountain sheep. These animals were an important source of food for the upcoming winter and were also used for clothing, tools and weapons. The women dried the meat and tanned the hides, which were used for making winter clothing.

The Caribou Hunters

The Subarctic peoples used deadfalls, snares, spears and bows and arrows to hunt a variety of animals, including musk-oxen, moose and smaller animals such as hares, beavers, muskrats and porcupines. But for many Subarctic groups, caribou were the most important animals.

The caribou travelled in huge herds. Each spring they migrated north to give birth to their calves. In the fall they headed south to their winter feeding grounds in the forests. They used the same routes year after year. The enormous size and predictable routes of the herds made them easier prey than many animals. And because caribou are big animals, the hunters could reap a better yield for their efforts — killing one large animal was more efficient than having to find many smaller ones.

Men, women and children joined in a communal hunt. They would drive the caribou into wooden surrounds or corrals or wait until the caribou were slowed down as they crossed a river or lake, then spear one and drag it to shore.

In winter, people required extra calories to combat the cold. The hunting was more difficult, and if the hunters didn't find enough food (meat and fat) to provide the necessary calories, their families would perish.

Although hunting was the main source of food, the Subarctic peoples also fished and gathered from the wild. The men caught sturgeon, whitefish, trout and pike. The women gathered blueberries, huckleberries, raspberries and Saskatoon berries.

Caribou uses

Fresh caribou meat was boiled or roasted and enjoyed around the campfire. Meat was also cut into strips and dried for later use. Some of the dried meat was pounded into a coarse powder and mixed with fat to make pemmican, a high-energy source of food eaten while on the trail. But food wasn't the only use the caribou was put to.

The hair and flesh were scraped from raw caribou hides. Then the hides were softened and preserved by soaking them in a mixture of water and caribou brains and by scraping, stretching, rubbing and finally smoking them. Once the hides were tanned in this way, they could be turned into a number of useful items, including coats, parkas, leggings, dresses, bags, moccasins, mittens and knife sheaths.

Strips of caribou leather were cut into thongs called "babiche" and used to lace snowshoes, tie down loads, build snares, make nets and pull toboggans.

Antlers and bones were adapted into tools such as knives, bone beamers (used to remove hair from a hide) and bone fleshers (used to scrape flesh from a hide).

Caribou sinew was made into thread for sewing garments and tents.

The intestine was used as a container to store fat and grease or pemmican.

Bags used to store meat were often made from caribou leg skins. The head skins of young caribou were sometimes used to make hoods for children's parkas.

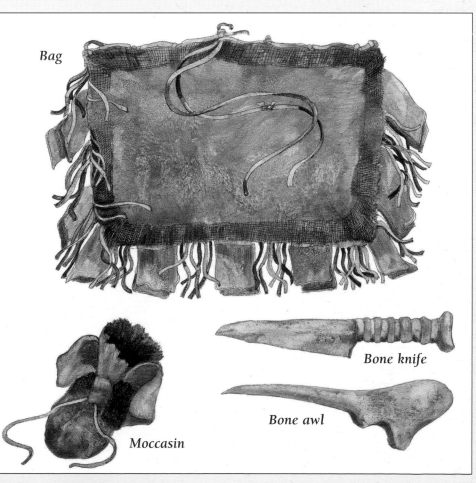

Bag

Bone knife

Bone awl

Moccasin

Transportation

In summer, the Subarctic peoples travelled in canoes covered with lightweight birchbark. They took along repair kits (extra bark, spruce root and spruce gum) to patch any holes.

But much travel was on foot. People carried large loads, including small children, on their backs. Women in particular carried heavy loads when camps were moved. Some groups also used dogs as pack animals.

Winter travel was made possible by snowshoes, which were made in a number of different shapes and sizes. The frame was made from wood laced with babiche (leather thongs). The large surface of the snowshoe kept the walker from sinking into deep, powdery snow. Some elongated styles were up to 2 m (6 1/2 ft.) long. These very large snowshoes were used by a hunter for running over unbroken snow.

Toboggans were used to carry loads in winter. Early toboggans were made out of the leg skins of caribou or moose. Later, wood was used. To make the upturned ends, planks were steamed and bent and lashed into position until dry. The long, thin toboggans slid easily over the snow, even with a heavy load of household belongings. They were usually pulled by the women. Dogs were not used to pull the toboggans until after the Europeans arrived with larger breeds of dogs.

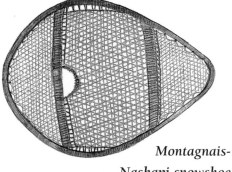

Montagnais-Naskapi snowshoe

Gwich'in snowshoe

Games

The children played a game of ring-and-pin. A player held the needle-like pin near the blunt end and swung the rest up and out. The object was to put the needle through a slit in the flat piece of hide.

Spiritual Beliefs

People asked shamans for help when they were sick or to help fight against spells put on them by their enemies. The shaman called on the spirits for aid.

In the eastern Subarctic, the shaman would isolate himself inside a tent to perform the shaking-tent rite. This rite took place after dark, and observers could witness strange animal noises and flickering lights coming from the shaking tent as the shaman communicated with the spirit world.

Hunters believed that the spirits of the animals watched them. If the animals were offended in any way, they would not offer themselves to be caught again. The killing of a bear was especially important and required the hunter to show his respect. He would honour the bear by placing its skull on a tree overlooking the water. Survival in the Subarctic was difficult, and the success of a hunt was often crucial.

Boys set out on a vision quest to acquire a guardian spirit (often an animal) that would help them during the hunt or in times of need. The people believed guardian spirits were capable of bringing about good or evil. A girl's behaviour during puberty was critically important in this regard. If she did not observe the correct rituals and taboos, she risked offending the animal spirits, and then the whole community could suffer.

Trade

The peoples traded tanned hides, clothing, meat and copper for making tools in exchange for things they needed. In the western Subarctic, the people traded with coastal peoples for dentalium shells and eulachon oil. Groups in the eastern Subarctic traded furs with their neighbours to the south for tobacco and other items.

Clothing

The women sewed clothing from animal hides. Winter clothing was often made from furred caribou hides. The caribou's hollow fur trapped air to provide insulation. For summer clothing, caribou or moose hides were dehaired and tanned. It took seven to ten moose or caribou skins to make an outfit for one person.

The basic outfit for people of the eastern Subarctic consisted of a knee-length shirt, breechclout, leggings and moccasins. A parka was added in winter. There was little difference between men's and women's clothing, except that the women's skirts were longer. In the western Subarctic, the parka was enlarged to accommodate a child on the mother's back. Most people of the western Subarctic wore a two-piece outfit consisting of a lower garment that combined pants and moccasins, and a long-sleeved top. The top was pointed in front and back for the men and straight across at the front for the women, like the Gwich'in summer clothing pictured below.

Moose skin was often used for moccasins because it is thick and strong. Moccasins and mittens were embroidered with porcupine quillwork in floral or geometric designs. Fur trim was often used for extra warmth and for decoration.

IROQUOIANS OF THE EASTERN WOODLANDS

Southeastern Ontario was, and still is, the home of the peoples who speak different dialects of the Iroquoian language. (Some of the groups were originally from the area, while others moved there after the American Revolutionary War, in the 1780s.)

At that time, southeastern Ontario was a mix of rolling hills, lakes, rivers and forests. The peoples lived in settled villages. They hunted and gathered as well as cultivating crops. They were skilled farmers, harvesting an abundance of food. They also developed a complex government.

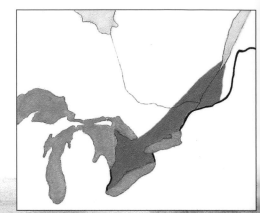

The peoples lived in longhouses, with sometimes five to six families in each. A large village might have as many as a hundred longhouses.

The village site was carefully selected. The location had to be easy to defend and discourage enemy attack. An example would be a hilltop, with a swamp or marsh at the base. The site also had to be near areas of rich soil for the crops, a forest for both building materials and firewood, and an adequate supply of fresh water for drinking and irrigating the crops.

Surrounding the houses were up to three rows of pointed posts called palisades. There was only a narrow entranceway into the village. In some villages, sentries on platforms or watchtowers kept watch for surprise raids from hostile groups.

The Iroquoian village of Hochelaga, when explorer Jacques Cartier first visited it in 1535, had about fifty longhouses with a population of fifteen hundred people, and was surrounded by triple palisades and extensive cornfields.

The longhouses were rectangular with barrel-shaped roofs. Arched poles running the length of the house were covered with cedar, ash, elm, spruce or fir bark. Houses varied from 20 m (65 ft.) to 60 m (200 ft.) long.

The interior of a longhouse was divided into family compartments. Sleeping platforms ran along the walls. Four or five cooking fires, one for every two families, burned in a row down the centre of the house.

The League of the Six Nations

Long before Canada's Confederation in 1867, five of the Eastern Woodlands nations joined together to form a confederacy (a political and military alliance). Started in the fourteenth or fifteenth century, this confederacy was at first made up of five nations — the Ganiengehaga, Cayuga, Onondaga, Oneida and Seneca. Then, in the 1700s, a sixth group, the Tuscarora, joined the confederacy, which came to be known as the League of the Six Nations.

The people of the League were grouped into nine clans: Turtle, Eel, Beaver, Bear, Deer, Wolf, Snipe, Hawk and Heron. The matron (clan mother) of each family within the clan selected a sachem (chief) to represent her family. In all, fifty sachems sat on a Grand Council and drafted the laws of the League. Although the sachems were men, it was the women who put them in power and could also remove them if they did not do their job satisfactorily.

The League was grounded on democratic principles. All important issues were discussed, and decisions were made when the majority of sachems were in agreement.

The main meetings of the Grand Council were held at Onondaga, south of Lake Ontario near what is now Syracuse, New York. There, the Council fire and the confederacy's records were kept. This Council house served as a representation of all the groups that came under the League's protection, with the Onondaga people being at the centre of the house, the Ganiengehaga guardians of the eastern door, the Seneca guardians of the western door and the Oneida and Cayuga standing on guard to the north and south.

The Wendat, Neutral, Erie and Tionontati peoples also formed a confederacy, in the late 1500s. The Wendat confederacy had eight clans, each with a war chief and a civil chief.

Gayanashagowa, or Great Law of Peace

According to a story often recited at ceremonial events, there was a time of great war among Iroquoian peoples. For many years, much blood was shed and many people lost their lives. During this time of constant war, two people, Deganawideh (known as The Peacemaker) and Hiawatha, began to talk of peace.

After many years of talk and negotiation, they succeeded in bringing together the five nations into a league. This league was founded on the Gayanashagowa, or Great Law of Peace.

The Great Law of Peace is a philosophy built on the ideas of peace, harmony and freedom. Under this law, individuals are seen as members of one family, which acts with one body, one mind and one heart.

Wampum belts were used to document agreements, treaties and important ceremonial events. They were made from shells that were hand-drilled, then polished. Elders entrusted with the history of the confederacy could recite it word for word using the belts as memory aids.

The fifty sachems of the confederacy were listed on a condolence cane (right). It is a symbol of authority and is still used today.

The symbol of the League of the Six Nations was, and still is, a pine tree. The roots of the Tree of Peace spread out in all directions. Anyone desiring peace has only to follow the roots to find the shelter of the great peace. At the top, an eagle stands on guard to protect all those who take shelter under it.

Feeding a Village

The peoples of the Eastern Woodlands were among the few Aboriginal groups who grew food crops as well as fished, hunted and gathered. They practised slash-and-burn agriculture, in which trees and brush are burned and the soil is fertilized by the ash. To clear the land, they first removed a ring of bark from a tree, then burned the base of the tree to make it easier to chop down. Once the land was cleared, the women prepared the soil for planting.

The main crops were maize (corn), beans and squash. The people referred to these as the "Three Sisters" or "Our Supporters." The plants were highly compatible, and the farmers wisely took advantage of this by growing them together. The corn stalks provided a natural support for the beans to climb up, while the squash plants growing close to the ground smothered the weeds.

Maize was the staple of their diet. In the fall, enough corn was dried and preserved to feed the entire village for the winter. A nutritious corn soup was made by grinding the dried kernels into cornmeal and then cooking it. The Wendat and other woodlands peoples even made an early form of popcorn. The Wendat called it "ogarita." The cornhusks were woven or braided into masks, mats, slippers and dolls.

To add variety to their meals, wild fruit, berries, roots, herbs and nuts were gathered and preserved for the winter. The peoples also collected sap from maple trees and boiled it down into maple syrup or sugar.

Ceremonies

Ceremonies were very important to people who depended on agriculture. The Seed Planting, Strawberry, Blackberry, Bean, Green Corn, Little Corn and Harvest festivals were held to thank the spirits for a bountiful harvest and ensure their aid with next year's crop. The ceremonies were held in the same order every year to mark the stages and cycle of planting and harvest.

False Face Society

Both the Haudenosaunee and the Wendat had groups, or "societies," that helped cure sicknesses caused by evil spirits. Members of the Haudenosaunee False Face Society wore a variety of face masks in their healing rituals — for example, a Smiling mask, a Hanging Lip mask, a Spoon Mouth mask. After the sick person recovered, he would join the group and make his own mask. He would "see" a special face in a dream and then carve it into a living basswood tree while burning tobacco at the same time. This ensured that the good spirit of the tree transferred to the mask.

During the Midwinter Ceremony, the Haudenosaunee False Face Society would travel to each longhouse to perform a purifying ritual. The ritual consisted of rubbing snapping turtle rattles against the

A snapping turtle rattle

door of the house, extinguishing the fire, stirring the ashes and then blowing them onto the occupants of the house. The villagers offered gifts of tobacco or corn mush to the False Faces for their services.

At times the False Face Society was assisted by the Husk Face Society, which acted as their messengers. Members of the Husk Face Society wore masks braided from dried cornhusks. Out of respect for the Haudenosaunee, their sacred masks are not shown here.

Games

Lacrosse is a ball game played by the Haudenosaunee and other groups. Players pass and catch a ball using a stick that has a shallow net at one end. The object of the game is to get the ball into the other team's net. It is a game of skill and endurance, but for many groups it was also thought to be a gift from the creator and had spiritual significance.

Transportation

Dugout and elm-bark canoes transported people and goods for trading. The canoes could hold a lot, but they were rather clumsy and unstable in rough water.

When on foot, people carried heavy bundles and baskets with the aid of a tumpline (a carrying strap).

During winter, snowshoes and toboggans allowed people to cross deep snow and frozen lakes.

Men leave their elm-bark canoes and carry their goods using tumplines.

ALGONQUIANS OF THE EASTERN WOODLANDS

The eastern woodlands were also the homeland of a diverse group of peoples who spoke one of the Algonquian languages. Their land stretched from Lake Superior and Lake Huron, west almost to the plains, east to the Atlantic Ocean, north into what is now northern Ontario and south below today's border with the United States. The land was mixed, with rolling hills, lakes, rivers, streams and forests.

Like the Iroquoians, a few Algonquian groups planted corn, beans and squash. But most survived by hunting, trapping, fishing and gathering plants from the wild. Wild rice played an important part in the diet of some groups. Here Ojibwe people harvest wild rice, a grass that grows in marshes and lakes. Properly dried and stored, wild rice lasted for a long time and could be eaten in winter when game was scarce.

Several families set up camp near a lake or marsh and took on different tasks. Some gathered wild rice from the lake. Others stayed at the camp to process the rice.

The men used long poles to pull their birchbark canoes through the water while the women knocked the grains of rice into the bottom of the canoes.

Algonquians of the Eastern Woodlands
Abenaki
Anissinapek (Algonkin)
Beothuk
Maliseet (Malécite)
Mi'kmaq (Micmac)
Odawa (Ottawa)
Ojibwe (Ojibway)

Domed or conical wigwams were made by covering a frame of poles with skins, woven mats or sheets of birchbark. (Wigwam comes from the Algonquian word "wigwaus," which means "birchbark.")

At the camp, the wild rice was processed. First, it was laid out on a birchbark sheet to dry in the sun. Then it was dried further by parching it over a fire. The dry rice was put into a pit lined with skins, and people took turns stomping on it to remove the outer husks. Finally, the rice was placed in a flat basket and tossed into the air to winnow it. The heavier grains fell back into the basket while the light husks blew away.

When needed, the rice was boiled in water and seasoned with berries or maple sugar. Excess rice was traded with neighbouring groups for squash, corn or beans.

People of the Birch

Birch trees grew in most parts of the lands of the Algonquian-speaking peoples. The trees were made into a number of useful items, such as canoes, homes and containers.

The bark was a particularly useful material — it is thin, tough and water-resistant. A sheet of bark was removed from the tree, often in one piece. This pliable bark could be shaped and moulded.

Canoes

The first step in making a canoe was to carefully peel a large piece of bark from a birch tree. (Sometimes bark from two small trees was sewn together.) Next a frame was built. The bark, which had been soaked in water, was laid out flat on the ground, and the frame was set on top. The bark was wrapped up and over the frame and held in place with stakes and ropes. The covering was sewn in place with split spruce roots. Bent ribs were inserted. The seams were sealed inside and out with spruce gum mixed with grease to make the canoe waterproof. The finished canoe was light but sturdy.

Homes

Overlapping sheets of birch or elm bark were wrapped over a framework of poles to make a rain-proof wigwam. Smoke from a fire in the centre of the wigwam rose through a hole at the top. The people slept on fur hides laid over a layer of fir boughs and stored their belongings around the edges of the wigwam.

Containers and Utensils

Drinking cups, boxes, trays, dishes and buckets were all made from birchbark. The buckets were used to carry water or collect sap from maple trees to make maple sugar. Birchbark boxes were often decorated with designs. Some had designs cut into the outer layer of the bark.

Other birchbark uses

Raincoats

A sheet of birchbark served as a raincoat when needed.

Moose calls

A hunter rolled a piece of birchbark into a cone to create a megaphone. By blowing into the small end of the cone, he could imitate the sound of a moose. If a moose was in the area, it would investigate the source of the sound.

Torches

Birchbark has a flammable wax coating, which makes it burn brightly. To make a torch, a piece of birchbark was rolled up and inserted into the split end of a stick. The men used the torches to attract fish close enough to their canoes to be speared.

Art

A thin layer of birchbark was folded several times and then bitten with the teeth. When it was unfolded and held up to the light, the beautiful design in the bark was revealed.

Hunting

The Algonquian-speaking peoples lived in small groups of twenty-five to forty people and moved with the seasons in search of game. Hunters knew the animals' migration patterns and followed them closely. They knew when the waterfowl were migrating in the spring and fall and when the fish were plentiful in the lakes and rivers. Still, finding enough food to survive required skill and resourcefulness.

Hunters used spears and bows and arrows to hunt animals such as buffalo, moose, caribou, deer, elk, bear, beaver, rabbits and porcupines. They were also trappers skilled in the use of snares and deadfalls. A snare is a hidden noose that can snag an unsuspecting animal that steps into it. A deadfall is a trap made of logs. A piece of meat is tied on a bait stick and set under a propped-up log. When the animal tugs on the meat, the propped log

drops on the animal's head or back, killing it. Fish and birds were also an important part of some groups' diets.

In winter, the hunters would look for moose tracks in the snow and follow the animal on snowshoes until they found it, often sunk in the snow because of its weight. Unable to escape, the moose was easy prey. Toboggans were used to haul the meat back to the camp.

Gathering

Plants gathered from the wild added to the peoples' diets and provided them with vitamins and medicines. The blueberry plant, for example, was made into a tea for headaches by the Ojibwe and into a tonic by the Odawa. Blueberry leaves and roots were boiled in water and the liquid applied to sore joints by the Mi'kmaq. Other berries were dried for food during the lean winter months.

Clothing

The women made clothing out of the hides of deer, caribou or moose. First, they removed the hair from the skins and scraped off the fat. Then the hide was soaked, stretched and smoked to tan it. They used a bone awl to make holes and caribou or deer sinew to sew the clothes together.

Everyday wear included a shirt, breechclout and leggings for the men. The women wore dresses with separate sleeves. The sleeves could be taken off in warm weather or for more flexibility. A fur robe was added in winter, often made of strips of rabbit fur woven together. The women often decorated clothes, hats and mittens with geometric designs made from dyed porcupine quills and moose hair embroidery.

Ceremonies and Spiritual Beliefs

The Algonquian-speaking peoples believed that all things had a spirit, including the plants, rocks and animals. This meant that all things must be treated with respect. If, for instance, a hunter was disrespectful to the animal he caught, he would not be successful in his next hunt. For a people whose very existence depended on hunting, certain rituals, such as saving the bones of animals and hanging them on a tree, were their way of showing respect to the animal.

Young men and women went on a vision quest to find a helping spirit who would assist them in the hunt and in other parts of their lives. In some areas, the candidate underwent rigorous training and fasting before embarking on the quest. The individual saw their helping spirit in a vision or a dream.

Shamans also went on vision quests, but their training was much more intense and their helping spirits were more powerful. Shamans performed curing rites. They began by putting themselves into a trance, whereupon their guardian spirit took over. The spirit was able to see the object that was causing the patient's distress. A tube was placed on the affected area and the foreign object sucked out of the body.

Tobacco was used as an offering to the spirits in the hopes they would listen to the prayers of the people and look favourably upon them. Singing and drumming were also a means of expressing gratitude to the spirits.

Games

Snowsnake was a winter game that required strength and a good eye. A long, sloping trough was dug in the snow and then iced down. Players threw special javelin-like sticks as far as they could along the trough. The player who threw the stick the farthest was the winner. Highly skilled snowsnake players could throw their sticks more than 1.5 km (1 mi.).

ABORIGINAL PEOPLES AFTER CONTACT

For thousands of years, Aboriginal peoples lived in the traditional ways you have read about so far. But then things changed. Europeans began to cross the Atlantic in search of a new, faster route to the riches of the Orient. But instead of a new route, they found a "new world" and came into contact with its inhabitants — the Aboriginal peoples. Over hundreds of years, contact with Europeans would dramatically change the way Aboriginal peoples lived.

First Contact

Around 1100, in what is now called Newfoundland, the Beothuk people witnessed strange ships entering their waters. The ships had large sails, high prows and, on each side, lines of men rowing. The Norse (also known as Vikings) had arrived, and they soon made contact with the Beothuks.

At first the Norse appeared friendly, and the Beothuks traded with them. But before long communications broke down and battles erupted between the newcomers and the Aboriginals. The Norse referred to the Beothuk people as Skraelings, which means "little wretches."

The Norse left, and it would be many years before any Europeans again visited North America. When the Europeans *did* return, the Beothuks would suffer from the diseases that the newcomers brought and the disruption of their usual hunting patterns by settlers eager for land. In some cases, a bounty was paid to anyone who would kill a Beothuk. By the early 1800s, the Beothuk had been driven to extinction as a people.

Indian or Aboriginal?

In 1492 Christopher Columbus, searching for a westward route to the Orient, landed in the Caribbean, nearly half a world away from his destination. Columbus, believing he was in the Indies (as Europeans called the area of China, Japan and India), mistakenly named the people "Indians." The name stuck and came to be applied to all Aboriginal peoples of the Americas. In recent years, the peoples of Canada have preferred to be called Aboriginal people, Native people or First Nations.

The Explorers Arrive

In 1497, just five years after Christopher Columbus first sailed to America, John Cabot landed in the vicinity of Newfoundland or Labrador. Although he was anxious to trade for furs, he was unable to establish contact with the Aboriginal people of the area. He laid claim to territory belonging to Aboriginal people in the name of the King of England and returned home full of stories about the abundant fish. Fishermen travelled to the area. They traded with the Aboriginal people, exchanging goods for furs.

Years later, French explorer Jacques Cartier explored eastern Canada. On his first trip, in 1534, he erected a cross on the Gaspé Peninsula claiming the territory for France. The land he claimed for France was the territory of Aboriginal people.

Kanata/Canada

The word Canada comes from the Wendat-Haudenosaunee word "kanata." French explorer Jacques Cartier heard the term from two Aboriginal youths. Kanata means "our village." The young men were referring to their village of Stadacona. But Cartier took up the term and applied it to the whole country. Kanata later became Canada.

By coincidence, a group of Haudenosaunee led by Chief Donnacona was fishing in the area. Donnacona made it clear to Cartier that he disapproved of the cross, but Cartier told him he was only leaving a marker to help him find his way back. Cartier returned to France with two of Donnacona's sons. Their stories of the riches of Canada prompted Cartier to return the next year.

On the 1535 trip, Cartier sailed up the St. Lawrence River to Stadacona (now Quebec City), the village where Donnacona was chief. The village was home to 500 people. Despite Chief Donnacona's protests, Cartier continued on to the even larger village of Hochelaga (now Montreal).

The following spring, Cartier returned to France with captives. He kidnapped Chief Donnacona and nine others to show them to the King of France. Chief Donnacona later died in France.

Jacques Cartier erects a cross on Aboriginal land in 1534.

The First Settlers

In 1605 Samuel de Champlain helped found Port-Royal in what is now Nova Scotia. It was the first permanent French settlement in Canada. French fishermen and settlers traded goods, such as axes, knives and pots, with the Mi'kmaq people in exchange for beaver furs. At that time there was a great demand in Europe for beaver fur to make into hats and coats.

In 1608 Champlain travelled down the St. Lawrence River and built a fort at what is now Quebec City. The fort soon became the center of the fur trade. There, Aboriginal people traded furs for European goods, such as knives, pots and blankets.

With the help of Aboriginal guides, the fur trade gradually spread westward. It would last for many years and bring many changes to the Aboriginal way of life.

The fur trade brought Aboriginal people into contact with Europeans.

Contact on the West Coast

In 1741 Vitus Bering, a Danish explorer in the service of the Russian navy, discovered sea otters along the Alaska coast. The news spread like wildfire back to Russia. Traders were anxious to obtain the luxurious, warm pelts from Aboriginal peoples in Alaska and British Columbia. The furs would fetch goodly sums in Russia and China.

Spanish explorer Juan Pérez Hernández traded with the Nuu-chah-nulth for sea otter pelts in 1774, as did Captain James Cook four years later. To welcome Cook, Chief Maquinna sent canoes to greet Cook's ship. A shaman stood on the bow of one canoe throwing eagle down (feathers) upon the water as a sign of friendship.

Cook was amazed at what shrewd traders the Nuu-chah-nulth were. They wanted metal, such as iron or brass, in exchange for sea otter pelts and would settle for nothing less. Cook did not know that Aboriginal peoples were very experienced at trading with one another.

In 1792 George Vancouver charted parts of the Pacific coast from California to Alaska. He took the liberty of renaming many of the Aboriginal places. He named Puget Sound after his lieutenant, Peter Puget, and Burrard Inlet after his friend, Sir Harry Burrard Neale.

Trade with the Europeans supplied the Northwest Coast peoples with new tools. European chisels made carving easier. Wealthy chiefs ordered carvings for ceremonial purposes, and many of those carvings last to this day, adding to the fame of the west coast carvers. But trade with the Europeans also changed Aboriginal lives for the worse. The Europeans brought with them fatal diseases, including smallpox. And many Aboriginal peoples set aside traditional hunting, fishing and gathering to hunt sea otters for trade. As a result, there were shortages of food for the winter,

MAQUINNA

Nuu-chah-nulth Chief Maquinna became a prominent middleman between the European traders and Aboriginal groups. Maquinna acquired a great deal of wealth in the process, wealth that he used to host elaborate potlatches. His name and status became renowned. He once invited the explorer George Vancouver to a feast. The guest committed the ultimate insult of declining the food he was offered and bringing his own food with him.

and entire villages went hungry.

Misunderstandings and insults often led to friction. In 1811 the British ship *Tonquin* lay at anchor in Clayoquot Sound. A Nuu-chah-nulth chief and a handful of his men came on board to trade their furs. The captain of the ship was Jonathan Thorn, an arrogant, rude man with a hair-trigger temper. It is believed that Thorn let his anger overcome him during the bartering process. He slapped the elderly chief across the face, then proceeded to throw him overboard. In retaliation, Captain Thorn and most of his crew were killed and the ship was seized. The next day the ship blew up — a crew member set fire to the ship's magazine and everyone on board was killed.

West coast carvers created totem poles and other carved objects that amazed the Europeans.

Forts and Explorers

Trade led to distrust and skirmishes in other parts of Canada, too. But the Europeans depended on Aboriginal people for furs. As long as the arrangement was profitable, there was no need to disrupt the Aboriginal way of life.

In the 1800s fur trading posts were established in the west by the Hudson's Bay Company and the North West Company. The companies needed water routes to bring the furs to their forts. To find these routes, they sent out explorers. But the explorers, while adventurous, knew nothing about living off the land. The solution was to hire Aboriginal guides. Aboriginal women played a key role on these trips, attending to food, repairing clothing and acting as translators.

Aboriginal guides travelled with Henry Kelsey, the first European to see the prairies, in 1690. Chief Attickasish guided Anthony Henday, who crossed the prairies in 1754. Matonabbee guided Samuel Hearne, who explored northern Canada in 1770–72.

Aboriginal guides led Henry Kelsey across the prairies in 1690.

◆ PROFILE ◆

MATONABBEE

Matonabbee was a Chipewyan chief who acted as a middleman between the traders at Hudson's Bay Company and the northern people who came to trade their furs.

Matonabbee guided Samuel Hearne overland to the Arctic Ocean in 1770–72. His knowledge of travel, hunting and living off the land made the expedition possible.

In 1793 Alexander MacKenzie set out for the second time to find a river route flowing from east to west, into the Pacific. MacKenzie and three other Europeans were guided by two Chipewyans. The group, along with a dog, set out by canoe from the Peace River for the Pacific Ocean. The trip was hard and dangerous. They travelled across the Rocky and Coast mountain ranges, portaged their canoes around rapids in the river and scaled sheer cliffs.

MacKenzie realized that local Aboriginal people could provide him with valuable information in his search. He received help from the Dunne-za, Tsay Keh Dene,

Wetsuwet'en and Dakelh-ne nations. He was advised to travel overland along the well-worn "grease trails" that led from the interior to the ocean. (For more about these trading trails, see page 11). When they reached the Pacific, the party was invited by the Nuxalk to a scrumptious feast.

MacKenzie succeeded in reaching the Pacific, but the route he had taken was not feasible as a trade route. After talking to the Nuxalk and Heiltsuk peoples, he came to realize captains James Cook and George Vancouver had already visited the area.

In 1806 Simon Fraser explored an unnamed river down to its mouth. The Musquem people living at the river mouth would have been surprised to learn their river had been "discovered." The river was later named the Fraser River.

Missionaries

Starting in the seventeenth century, missionaries arrived in Canada. They had been sent to look after the religious life of the Europeans — and to convert the Aboriginal peoples to Christianity. Early missionaries travelled by canoe to reach the Aboriginal peoples. But the language barrier meant they had little success.

Catholic and, later, Protestant missionaries tried to get Aboriginal peoples to reject their sacred beliefs and practices. The missionaries set out to rid the people of their ceremonies, such as the Sun Dance of the Plains and the potlatch of the Northwest Coast. They wanted to make the Aboriginal people more like the Europeans. As time went on, this attitude would damage and nearly destroy Aboriginal traditions.

Disease

Traders, soldiers and missionaries brought with them diseases such as cholera, leprosy, malaria, measles, scarlet fever, smallpox, tuberculosis, typhoid fever and whooping cough. The Aboriginal people had no immunity to these diseases, and as a result, up to three-quarters of them were wiped out in many areas. Even an ordinary cold could prove deadly.

Epidemics swept through Aboriginal groups. It is estimated that when Europeans first arrived in Canada, there were approximately 350 000 Aboriginal people. By 1867 the Aboriginal population was about one-third of what it had been, and disease played a big role in the decline.

European diseases devastated the Aboriginal population.

More Settlers

European explorers and fur traders built forts, and the forts attracted settlers from Europe who wanted to stay on and make the new country their home. These European settlers were the most serious threat yet —

their arrival signalled the end of the traditional way of Aboriginal life.

In eastern Canada, the settlement at Quebec City, started in 1608, was growing. On the prairies, a

settlement grew up at Fort Garry, near what is now Winnipeg, in the early 1800s. On the west coast, settlers began arriving in Coast Salish territory at what is now Victoria and New Westminster in the mid-1830s.

During the fur trade, Aboriginal and European people had worked side by side as trading partners. The settlers, however, were another matter. They were in direct competition with Aboriginal people for land.

The settlers wanted ownership of the land so they could clear and plough it to grow crops. They began to see the Aboriginal people as obstacles or nuisances. In the late 1800s and early 1900s, Aboriginal peoples were moved off their land and onto reserves. The settlers took their land.

Aboriginal women gather berries outside Fort Victoria, B.C.

The Métis

The Métis were the descendants of Aboriginal peoples and Europeans who had intermarried. Fur traders relied on the Métis to supply them with pemmican. The Métis men hunted the buffalo, from which the women made pemmican. The men also farmed, trapped and traded furs.

By the mid-1800s, 10 000 Métis lived in the area near what is now Winnipeg. But in 1869 the Canadian government made plans to offer the land to English settlers. The Métis were not consulted.

Prime Minister John A. Macdonald sent surveyors to divide the land into plots. Métis leader Louis Riel informed the surveyors that they had no right to survey Métis land and sent them packing. In response, Macdonald appointed a governor to manage the affairs at Fort Garry, the heart of the Red River settlement.

A rebellion broke out, led by Riel. The Métis captured Fort Garry and declared a new government

for the area — a Métis government led by Riel.

The Métis drew up a list of eighteen rights they wanted guaranteed, including the protection of their land and a voice in the government. A man named Thomas Scott, who had been taken prisoner when the fort was captured by the Métis, managed to escape and proceeded to mount a counter-revolution against Riel. Scott was recaptured, court-martialled and

executed. The Canadian government was incensed. They sent the army to capture Riel, who fled to the United States.

Many Métis left Manitoba and moved to Saskatchewan. There, the government once again began to survey their lands. In desperation, the Métis sent a delegation led by Gabriel Dumont to find Riel and ask him to return.

In 1885 Riel led his people in a second rebellion, this time in Saskatchewan. Riel formed a new government and picked Gabriel Dumont as leader of his 400 Métis fighters. The Métis proceeded to cut telegraph lines, raid supplies and launch an attack at Duck Lake. The next battle, at Batoche, however, ended in the defeat of the Métis, who were outnumbered and outgunned.

Two Cree chiefs, Poundmaker and Big Bear, tried to stop their warriors from joining in the rebellion. Despite their efforts to maintain peace, they were tried and found guilty of felony and treason and sentenced to a term in jail.

◆ PROFILE ◆

LOUIS RIEL

Louis Riel was born in 1844 in the settlement of Red River. An educated spokesman, he was fluent in both French and English and a born leader. He championed Métis rights, especially land rights. He fought injustice at the hands of the government and ended up giving his life for his beliefs. In 1885 he was convicted of treason and hanged.

The Indian Act

The rift between the Aboriginal people and the Europeans widened. The government of Canada stepped in to take control and introduced, in 1876, the Indian Act. The goal of this Act was to assimilate the Aboriginal peoples — to make them give up their traditional ways and blend into the non-Aboriginal population.

Over the years, the Indian Act was amended (changed) forty-two times. For example, when Aboriginal people began raising money to hire lawyers to defend their claim to the land, the Indian Act was amended. They now required the government's permission to hire lawyers.

Aboriginal people who refused to renounce their official Aboriginal status were denied certain rights, such as the right to a high school education, to vote, buy land or serve on juries. The Act went so far as to deny Aboriginal people the right to use fish weirs, to own powerboats and to sell fish.

Rather than assimilating the Aboriginal peoples, the Act made Canada into a two-tiered system based on race. Aboriginal people who refused to give up their "Indian" status became wards of the government with few rights, while other Canadians were citizens and had full rights.

The Indian Act is still in force today, although its fate remains uncertain. Most Aboriginal people agree that the Indian Act has not served their people well. However, some still see a role for Canadian government involvement in Aboriginal affairs, while others are fighting for self-government. Time will tell. As with Canadians in general, people of Aboriginal descent have different views on the best path to the future.

JAMES GLADSTONE

In 1958 James Gladstone, from the Blood Reserve in Alberta, became the first Aboriginal person appointed to the Senate of Canada. Ironically, Senator Gladstone did not have the right to vote in federal elections until 1960 or in his home province of Alberta until 1965 because of his Aboriginal status. He was a strong champion of Aboriginal rights.

The Banning of Traditional Customs and Governments

Soon after Confederation in 1867, the newly formed Canadian government began to outlaw Aboriginal traditions, such as the potlatch. At the potlatch, titles are received and spiritual ceremonies and political events are held. The potlatch served as a form of government for a number of the peoples of the Northwest Coast. In 1884 the potlatch was banned, and anyone participating in a potlatch could be jailed for up to six months. In 1921, in defiance of the ban, a potlatch was held in Alert Bay on Vancouver Island. A group of elders was arrested and put in jail. Six hundred ceremonial pieces, such as robes, rattles and masks, were confiscated by the RCMP. The pieces

In residential schools, Aboriginal children were isolated from their families and their culture.

were sold to museums or ended up in the hands of collectors.

The bans were extended to many Aboriginal traditions. For example, in 1885 the federal government forbade Aboriginal peoples of the Plains from participating in the Sun Dance. As a result of banned customs, centuries of traditional cultural practices were almost wiped out.

In the 1920s the federal government jailed the traditional leaders of the League of the Six Nations. The RCMP ransacked their Council house and seized the records and wampum belts. The Canadian government dismissed the traditional leaders and replaced them with their own Indian Act council. Across Canada, Aboriginal groups were not allowed to choose their own band councils or set their own laws.

Residential Schools

The push to make Aboriginal people more like other Canadians continued. The government wanted Aboriginal people to abandon their past, their customs and their language. Starting in the 1880s, this push for assimilation took its saddest turn yet. Children as young as six years old were taken from their families and placed in the "care" of strangers at residential schools.

When the children arrived at residential school, their long hair was cut off, their names changed to more "Canadian-sounding" names, and they were punished or beaten if they spoke their own language. Some suffered mental, physical and sexual abuse from school authorities. They were seldom permitted to visit their parents. The parents and relatives were only allowed to visit for very short times, if at all.

For many years, children in residential schools often went hungry and spent the majority of their time doing menial chores. The little education they received at the school didn't prepare them to find jobs. And they were also robbed of the chance to learn traditional hunting and fishing skills. A few children never returned home but died mysteriously at the schools. Many of those who did return were damaged, and many had a hard time fitting into their traditional cultures.

Most residential schools were closed by the mid-1970s. The last residential school, located in Saskatchewan, was closed in 1996. On June 11, 2008, the prime minister of Canada issued an apology to the survivors of the residential schools.

Today and Tomorrow

Aboriginal people over the years have fought hard for their rights and for justice. But the Indian Act, the banning of customs, the loss of traditional lands, the residential schools and other policies of the Canadian government took their toll. Today, Aboriginal people still have higher levels of unemployment, lower incomes, the highest suicide rate in the country and a life expectancy ten years less than the rest of the population.

In the last half-century, new Aboriginal organizations have emerged to take up the battle. And the people themselves continue to press for their rights and justice. For example, in 1986 the Cree people of Quebec united to stop the Great Whale Project, a hydroelectric dam that would have flooded their lands.

Political organizations today

- The Assembly of First Nations represents Aboriginal people who are registered under the Indian Act (they are called "status Indians"), including those who have rights by treaty (called "treaty Indians").
- The Congress of Aboriginal People represents Aboriginal people who live off reserves or are Métis or belong to certain communities with strong Aboriginal ties.
- The Inuit Tapirisat of Canada represents Inuit people.
- The Métis National Council represents the Métis in Canada.

HAROLD CARDINAL

Harold Cardinal was angered by the Canadian government's refusal to listen to Aboriginal people. In 1969 he wrote *The Unjust Society* in response to the Canadian government's plan to do away with Aboriginal rights. Mr. Cardinal's harsh picture of the unjust treatment of Aboriginal people forced the government to reconsider its position. For his work, Harold Cardinal won the National Aboriginal Achievement Award for Lifetime Achievement in 2000.

They had already seen the effects of flooding as a result of a dam. In the 1970s the James Bay Hydroelectric Project had devastated the economy, culture and environment of the Cree and Inuit in the area. The flooding destroyed their villages and land and contaminated the fish with mercury, causing a major health risk for the Cree who relied on them for food. In 1986 the Cree worked with environmental groups and spent millions of dollars to stop the same thing from happening again.

National and local Aboriginal organizations began working for changes that would re-establish Aboriginal rights to the land and control over their own destinies.

Treaties and Land Claims

One big issue that remains to be resolved is treaties. A number of treaties were signed between the French and English and Aboriginal peoples before Canada became a country. Later, the government of Canada continued to sign treaties with Aboriginal peoples.

A treaty is a binding contract between two nations. To the Aboriginal people, treaties set out how the two nations would share the land. But the Europeans saw the treaties as a way to get Aboriginal people to give up their claim to the land. As Europeans saw it, once a treaty was signed, the Aboriginal people no longer had a right to their traditional lands. But Aboriginal people had a different view: signing a treaty did not mean they gave up their claim to their lands. They want the right to manage their own land and the resources, such as forests and minerals, that are a part of it.

◆ PROFILE ◆

DR. FRANK CALDER

Frank Calder became the first Aboriginal Cabinet Minister when he joined the B.C. Cabinet in 1972. He led several Aboriginal organizations and was outspoken in his belief that Aboriginal people had an ongoing claim to their ancestral lands. In 1996 he received a National Aboriginal Achievement Award for Lifetime Achievement, and in 1988 was made an Officer of the Order of Canada.

In British Columbia only fourteen treaties were signed, leaving in dispute the ownership of most of the province. In 1996 Dr. Frank Calder of the Nisga'a Nation filed a lawsuit against the province of B.C. over land claims. It argued that Aboriginal people had the right to their land under Canadian law. Six out of seven Supreme Court judges agreed. The Calder Case prompted the government to begin negotiating unsettled land claims across Canada. These negotiations continue today.

DOROTHY BETZ

Dorothy Betz was a driving force behind the development of Native Friendship Centres across Canada. The centres address the needs of Aboriginal people moving to cities by offering counselling and referral services in education, employment, health and housing. The centres played a key role in Aboriginal people's transition from the country to the cities by offering information and support to those coming and looking for work, as well as a place to socialize.

The flag of Nunavut features a red inukshuk, which is a guide for travellers and a marker of special places. The North Star represents the importance of elders and their leadership.

Environmental Issues

Aboriginal communities face problems with water quality that have been solved for most other Canadians. As many as 20 000 Aboriginal people across the country lack running water and adequate sanitation, and more than 100 communities do not have safe drinking water. Although there has been much talk about improving the situation, safe clean water and sanitation remain a big problem. Aboriginal peoples face other environmental issues, as well. For example, groups in northern Alberta are concerned about arsenic, lead and other toxins leaking into the Athabasca River from tailing ponds used to store waste from the mining of oil in the oil sands. More than 1600 birds have died after landing on the tailing ponds and becoming coated with oil. Deformed fish have been found in the Athabasca River. The Aboriginal people worry that pollution from the oil sands may be upsetting the balance of nature, putting at risk their traditional way of life, which is based on hunting, fishing and trapping. The pollutants have also been linked to health problems in humans, including cancers. The Aboriginal groups are working to publicize the problem and put an end to it.

Self-Government

As the original inhabitants of Canada, Aboriginal people claim the inherent right to govern themselves, rather than have another government impose laws on them. Today, Aboriginal people are seeking the restoration of self-government. They want to take control over their own education, health, finance, justice and housing programs, rather than have these dictated by the government of Canada. Progress is slowly being made. In 1999 the new territory of Nunavut,which is 80 per cent Inuit, was created. It has its own government, laws and courts.

The Nisga'a Nation in B.C. regained control over their own affairs in 2000. They now have a central government — the Nisga'a Lisims government. Elsewhere, Aboriginal peoples continue to press for more control over their lives and future.

One aspect of self-government that is particularly important for Aboriginal people is justice. Traditionally, Aboriginal children learned at an early age the difference between right and wrong and how to deal with each other with respect. Pressure from the community ensured wrongs were made right. For example, for serious offences, offenders could be banned from their community. There was no need for police and prisons.

In general, Aboriginal people believe in healing rather than in punishing the offender, which is why the prison system is alien to their values. Recently there has been a return to traditional Aboriginal methods, such as sentencing circles, to help heal people. A sentencing circle is made up of elders, family, friends, police, the victim and the offender. Decisions are made when everyone is in agreement. The rights of the victim and the needs of the offender are taken into consideration. The co-operation of the entire community is needed to support both the victim and the offender while healing takes place.

Cultural Renewal

Despite repeated attempts to ban traditional practices and assimilate Aboriginal people, Aboriginal culture did not disappear. Rather, it was held in sacred trust by the elders, who are now helping to rekindle traditional concepts and practices.

Today, centuries-old traditions — dances, songs and feasts — are being passed along to the young, providing them with a sense of cultural pride, community and purpose in life.

Traditional Aboriginal culture was based on spirituality, which was meant to be a guiding force in a person's life. Attempts to destroy this force have failed. The cultural bonds of Aboriginal people have not and never will be broken.

Declaration of Kinship and Co-operation

At a meeting on the land of the Coast Salish people in Vancouver in the summer of 1999, the Assembly of First Nations and the National Congress of American Indians met and signed this declaration.

We, the people, knowing that the Creator placed us here on Mother Earth as sovereign nations, and seeking to live in peace, freedom and prosperity with all humanity in accordance with our own traditional laws, are united in our sacred relationship with the land, air, water and resources of our ancestral territories. We are bound by common origin and history, aspiration and experience, and we are brothers and sisters, leaders and warriors of our nations …

From time immemorial, the lands that are now known as Canada and the United States of America have been, and continue to be, the sacred home of Indigenous Peoples and Nations.

While our Indigenous Peoples and Nations have distinct identities, cultures, languages and traditions, we have also been guided by many common purposes and beliefs, which have been shaped by many common experiences:

We have all retained the inherent right to self-determination. In shaping our own destinies we will remain faithful to the time-honoured traditions of our ancestors, and we will work to secure the greatest possible freedom, dignity and prosperity for our descendants;

We have all known ourselves as people who live in harmony with our environment and cherish and protect our traditional homelands;

We have all shared a belief that individuals and peoples must address each other in a spirit of respect and tolerance;

We have all experienced outside encroachment upon our traditional homelands, and we have striven to co-exist with other peoples and cultures in peace …

INDEX

The subgroup names that appear at the beginning of each of the seven major groups have not been indexed unless the name appears elsewhere in the text. For a list of subgroup names, see the green boxes on the following pages: Northwest Coast, page 7; Plateau, page 13; Plains, page 19; Arctic, page 25; Subarctic, page 31; Eastern Woodlands Iroquoians, page 37; Eastern Woodlands Algonquians, page 43.

Kids Books of ...
Bringing Canada and the World to Life

The Kids Book of CANADA — Barbara Greenwood

The Kids Book of CANADIAN HISTORY — Written by Carlotta Hacker · Illustrated by John Mantha

The Kids Book of Canadian Prime Ministers — Pat Hancock

The Kids Book of CANADA AT WAR — Written by Elizabeth MacLeod · Illustrated by John Mantha

The Kids Book of CANADIAN IMMIGRATION — Written by Deborah Hodge · Illustrated by John Mantha

The Kids Book of CANADIAN GEOGRAPHY — Briony Penn

The Kids Book of ABORIGINAL PEOPLES in Canada — Written by Diane Silvey · Illustrated by John Mantha

The Kids Book of BLACK CANADIAN HISTORY — Written by Rosemary Sadlier · Illustrated by Wang Qijun

The Kids Book of Canada's RAILWAY AND HOW THE CPR WAS BUILT — Deborah Hodge

The Kids Book of CANADIAN EXPLORATION — Written by Ann-Maureen Owens & Jane Yealland · Illustrated by John Mantha

The Kids Book of The Far North — Ann Love & Jane Drake

The Kids Book of CANADIAN FIRSTS — Valerie Wyatt

The Kids Book of GREAT CANADIANS — Written by Elizabeth MacLeod · Illustrated by John Mantha

The Kids Book of WORLD RELIGIONS — Written by Jennifer Glossop · Illustrated by John Mantha

The Kids Book of GREAT CANADIAN WOMEN — Written by Elizabeth MacLeod · Illustrated by John Mantha

Visit www.kidscanpress.com to take a look inside these books
and for more information.